RIVERS OF TIME

Rivers of Time

Photographs by
Dame Freya Stark

WITH AN INTRODUCTION BY
ALEXANDER MAITLAND

William Blackwood
1982

First published in 1982
by William Blackwood & Sons Ltd,
32 Thistle Street,
Edinburgh EH2 1HA

© Freya Stark 1982

No part of this book, photographs or text, may be reproduced in any form without the permission of the publisher, except for brief passages used for the purpose of criticism or review.

British Library Cataloguing in Publication Data

Stark, Freya
    Rivers of Time: Photographs by Dame Freya Stark.
    1. Near East — Description and travel — Pictorial work
    I. Title
    915.6'043   DS49.7

ISBN 0 85158 – 147 – 1

Printed by Johanns Graphics Ltd, Waterloo, Ontario, Canada

From Evening to the Morning

William Blackwood are grateful to Suomi La Valle for allowing them to use his photographic portrait of Dame Freya for the frontispiece of this book.

Foreword

Dame Freya Stark unites in one mind the traveller, the historian, the writer and the philosopher. The toughness of an explorer and the sensibility of an artist rarely concur in one person as they do in her. Margaret Lane wrote: 'About once in a century the small shores and moist airs of these inlands produce a traveller of genius, whose spirit is drawn to deserts, and burning suns, and who has the rare gift of being able to interpret the experience. Such a one is Freya Stark.'

Elements of her character have been consistent throughout her long life: a love of mountains has been with her from her early years of climbing with her godfather W. P. Ker in the Alps, when she first came to know danger and the nearness of death, to her expeditions into the Himalayas in her eighties; a stamina, a courage against indifferent health and a stubborn determination to reach her goal, be it some desert fastness or the building of a surprisingly large house and the designing of a magnificent landscaped garden on a bare hill in North Italy against all opposition; a preference for travelling alone which may partly explain how in her travel-writing she carries her readers so closely with her; an intoxicating disregard of bureaucracy, particularly Customs Officers; and, above all, an Olympian view of history and a sense of perspective not only on life but on landscape. This selection of her photographs is an impressive record of some of her travels and seems, perhaps, a mirror to the pictorial quality of her enduring prose.

It is an honour and a delight, for an admirer over many decades, to be able to pay a tribute.

John Murray

Contents

Foreword	vii
Introduction	xi
Photographs	
Lebanon, Palestine, Syria, Transjordan	1-48
Iraq, Kuwait	49-76
Persia	77-102
South Arabia	103-146
Turkey	147-187
Egypt	188-202

Introduction

Freya Madeline Stark was born in her parents' studio in Montmartre, 37 Rue Denfert Rochereau, on 31st January 1893. Her father, Robert Stark, was thirty-nine, Paris-based, a painter and sculptor who specialised in portraiture, landscape and animals. Her mother, Robert's first cousin, had been born and brought up in Florence. Vivacious, extrovert, an accomplished pianist and a skilled portrait-painter, Flora Madeline at thirty-one felt drawn to society and the warm south, whereas her husband instinctively sought peace and quiet, wandering in the Italian Alps or riding across Dartmoor on whose fringes he eventually built a house, Ford Park, near Chagford. A second daughter, Vera, was born in 1894. The Starks were careful to choose names for their children which could not be easily shortened. Freya (pronounced Fray-ah), of Norwegian origin — as in Conrad's story, *Freya of the Seven Isles* — recalled her father's Nordic ancestors who had settled in the southwest of England early in the eighteenth century. Madeline was the name of Freya's maternal grandmother, an eccentric aristrocrat who, despite having squandered most of her fortune, survived long into a dignified independent old age.

Freya's developing character reflected many of these sometimes conflicting, sometimes complementary, influences. In childhood, she had loved books and horses, the Dolomite valleys, the Venetian summer, the windswept heaths of Dartmoor, her father's studio, her mother playing Liszt or Chopin. As she grew older, her cheerful gregariousness and enjoyment of good conversation challenged the solitary contentment she had found, until then, in reading and lonely moorland walks.

The Starks' year continued to be divided between England and Italy, where they lived at Asolo, a tiny medieval city fifty kilometres northwest of Venice. Both girls spoke three languages, English, German and Italian, by the age of five. Freya remembers how each language had its own compartment: English was for Father; German for Granny; Italian for Mother. There were remarkably few confusions. The children alternated between the different grammars and vocabularies with ease. Freya's voice today represents the cultured English model; yet certain inflections remind one of her polyglot background and a lifetime spent, between her travels, mainly in Italy.

In 1906, a terrible accident occurred. Freya was scalped and nearly killed by a mechanical loom in her mother's silk-factory. She described the event in her first volume of autobiography, *Traveller's Prelude* (1950):

'. . . as I was standing with a mass of loose curling hair almost to my knees, the wind of a

steel shaft caught it. I was snatched up, revolving, with my head ground against the shaft and my feet floating horizontal. I know that it seemed a very long time: at each revolution my feet struck a wall or pillar and I wondered if my shoes were coming off. I felt no pain or even fright. Then Mario wrenched me out and carried me away; I saw terrified faces; heard the machinery coming to a standstill; felt a warmth trickling down my neck; saw my mother meeting me with panic in her eyes that I noticed even at that moment; and next I was on mattresses in the office and some doctor was sewing my eyelid into place. Half the scalp was torn away . . .'

Flora Stark believed her daughter's life was finished. However, after skilful surgery the wounds gradually healed and a bonnet and wig concealed the more permanent damage. Four of Freya's earliest poems, written between July and December 1908, contain poignant reminders of her loss. Thus, she sadly recollects 'the whispering breezes/Which hardly lift our hair'; and 'feeling that same hand upon my hair'; and, again, winds that blow, 'stirring my hair about me as I stand'. The Starks had long since abandoned Ford Park and the damp Dartmoor climate which Flora detested. Now they stayed firmly rooted in Asolo, in the Via Robert Browning, next door to an old friend, Herbert Young. They continued to visit the Dolomites where Young, a gifted amateur artist and photographer, would often join them, having bicycled from Asolo — a four-day journey — detouring off to a cathedral on the way, here and there visiting a church, sleeping in country inns or in the hedgerows. The gentle, blue-eyed Australian photographed Freya and Vera as children playing and dancing in the garden. In 1926, Young bequeathed Freya his Asolo house, where he died fifteen years later.

The 'Casa Freia' flanks the Loreggia Gate, a simple brick arch with tiled castellations; and its rolling lawns interspersed with shrubbery and fine trees, among them hornbeams, laurels and the cypresses which Young first introduced to Asolo, extend more than halfway down the hill. There, in later years, Freya would stroll arm-in-arm with Asolo's elderly priest and throw gay, cosmopolitan lunch-parties under the cedars.

In the autumn of 1911, she was sent to London to continue her education at Bedford College, Regent's Park. In April the same year, Freya had composed an affectionate sonnet to her mother, which revealed something of her sensitive, artistic, yet determined, character:

'Thus let my thoughts and actions reach their goal
Upon this world and draw the shining band
Of your fair influence as a comet scroll...'

She boarded with her mother's friend, Viva Jeyes, keeping a precise account of her expenses, acclimatising slowly to the traffic and the noise. Alone in strange surroundings, Freya reflected wistfully upon happier days spent with her father in high mountain valleys or on Dartmoor and mourned 'the old life that we knew to make so dear/Still with me in the distance . . .'. She compared these memories to currents, seen one autumn night near Battersea Bridge, ruffling 'the still surface' of the Thames. Stimulated by the crowded city, nevertheless inwardly resenting it, Freya identified with her vision of the quiet stream 'waiting eternity' and wrote:

'Above it the dark bridge a shadow throws
Lined with a double row of lamps; here glows
The traffic and a busy throng of feet;
And motors pass as flames along a wire,
The noise encircles like a rising fire
To waken the mad spirit of the street.'

Through Viva Jeyes, Freya met a dour Scots Professor of Literature, W. P. Ker, who became her adopted godfather; he instructed her in such diverse accomplishments as Dante's geography and the rudiments of mountaineering, and encouraged her to write. She walked through Regent's Park from Bedford College to London University where, as an extra-mural student, she attended Ker's popular lectures; she soon became deeply devoted to 'W. P.', the bald, bespectacled bachelor who was taciturn and shrewd, yet a warm-hearted confidant. Long after Ker's death, Freya confessed that, despite the difference in their ages, she might have gladly shared her 'rather dry old professor's' last remaining years, willingly sacrificing youthful dreams of romantic fulfilment for the stimulating pleasure of his company.

Besides nourishing Freya's literary aspirations, Ker probably also became a father-substitute and a symbol of the united family which she unconsciously sought. Robert, 'Pips' as the children used to call him after a pet terrier, and Flora had grown irreconcilably apart. After the First World War, Robert emigrated to Canada, where he ended his days in British Columbia, growing prize-winning apples, looked after by an old family retainer, Tom, and his wife, from Devon, who used to irritate their emancipated neighbours by referring to Robert as 'the master'.

It is strange that, having been brought up in

an artistic houshold, Freya should have been positively discouraged from taking up painting or sculpture; equally strange that she had received no encouragement either to write or play some musical instrument. Bits of tapestry, a little gilt box decorated by her as a child, drawings and pen-and-wash studies made during her later travels, all show clear evidence of artistic talent. The swing towards literature may have begun in the summer of 1908 when she wrote her earliest sentimental verses. In London, Ker helped her strengthen these fragile foundations, sternly criticising her poetry and essays. His advice was often cryptic — 'too many words'; however, on one occasion, in a rare expression of delight, he embraced her silently as he handed back a manuscript.

Their platonic friendship continued until Freya was thirty. Ker visited Italy each year, where he shared the Starks' mountain holidays. Freya, in turn, later visited Ker's sisters at their home in the Campsie Fells, near Glasgow. In 1923, during an ascent of the ice-mountain Monte Rosa, Ker died of a heart-attack. He was buried at Macugnaga, below the glittering peak 'sharp with spears of icicle and stone'. Freya scattered Alpine flowers, 'rose-frilled dianthus and the dark blue-bell', upon the grave; these and yellow lilies whose

'Wild and tender fragrance will recall
The happiness of our adventurous morns,
While Rosa's shining horns
Receive the night & morning, & the fall
Of her loud streams is steady to your ear —
Rough mountain voice to lull the mountaineer.'

In 1914, she returned to Italy without having obtained her degree. At Bologna, she trained briefly as a nurse and afterwards helped to care for wounded Italian troops at a tiny hospital in the hills within sight of the front line. The experience affected her deeply, and memories of the hospital and of exhausted soldiers sleeping in moonlight among the stones of a riverbed haunt her to this day. Once, inadvertently, she administered an overdose of anaesthetic and, fearing the worst, fainted; but the patient recovered and a young doctor brought Freya round, with the doubtful assurance that he and his colleagues had all killed somebody at one time or another during their careers!

After the war, her mind grew progressively more occupied with the East, in particular with the Arab world so powerfully evoked in carefully wrought Elizabethan prose by Charles Montagu Doughty, whose two-volumed *Travels in Arabia Deserta* had been given to her by Viva Jeyes. Freya had expected the 1400-page book to last a whole summer; however, she read it in a fortnight. And an old 1915 diary, used as a fairly robust. She dressed stylishly and wore a neat, bobbed wig. At first she rented rooms in the squalid native quarter of Baghdad and each day walked to work at the local newspaper. In due course, persuaded by friends, she moved to a pleasant, airy house overlooking the Tigris, where, by trimming her modest income, she managed to give small, weekly dinner-parties. She also began to travel. For *The Baghdad Times* she wrote a series of articles which the paper afterwards collected and published as *Baghdad Sketches*, her first book, in 1932. After Freya had been diverted from art by her parents, her first significant step towards a literary career came when Viva Jeyes introduced her to W. P. Ker. Ker provided Freya with the wherewithal to develop her craft. The second step, again initiated by Viva Jeyes, was the discovery of Doughty. Doughty's *Travels in Arabia Deserta* had excited her, focused her attention on the Middle East and inspired a lifelong fascination with the Arab world. The little symposium, *Baghdad Sketches*, carried Freya forward to a third, equally important, event.

The publisher, John Murray, read a manuscript describing journeys Freya had made in Luristan, *The Valleys of the Assassins* (1934). Murray published the work, which was immediately acclaimed as a record of outstanding personal achievement, no less than for its haunting portrayal of people and the 'enthralling substance' of the journeys themselves. Freya and John Murray became close friends, and a literary association began which has continued to flourish without interruption until the present day. The trends within Freya's life had resolved at last into a clearer pattern. Foremost of all, she was a writer. Travel in the Middle East provided inspiration, besides a wealth of material for her books.

In Arabia, her chief interest lay in the life and people of the remote townships bordering the desert, where she searched for evidence of Man's history, tracing the faint impress of his passage across those arid, inhospitable lands. She felt no overpowering urge to pit her physical and mental strengths against either the great deserts or the desert-dwellers themselves. She acknowledged the desert's challenge, without exulting in hardship for hardship's sake. Degrees of hunger, thirst and discomfort identified the desert profile, offering harsh experiences shared alike by every traveller, whether Bedouin or European. These Freya accepted unconditionally, according her portion no more, no less, importance than it deserved. Although she enjoyed well-cooked food and boasted a healthy appetite, when necessary she would fast without complaint. Once, at Garmrud, in Persia, she shared a tiny peasant supper of boiled tomatoes with three hungry companions, two of whom divided the same

Commonplace Book, contains the following extract from G. A. Welling, written in Freya's fine sloping hand of the mid-1920s: 'I think that even a professing Christian who knew the language & was familiar with Bedouin virtues, such as hospitality and manliness, could live among them.' Doughty had proved as much already; later English travellers, Gertrude Bell, T. E. Lawrence, would do the same.

The tiny green pocket-diary abounds in quotations describing Eastern travel: deserts, Iraq, the Euphrates. References to the Arabs occur repeatedly: their 'quick-eyed pagan' appearance, customs, mode of travel, religious observances. Interleaved with fragments of her poetry and gardening-notes, are a meticulous daily record of her temperature throughout an illness, and pages of Arabic vocabulary copied out by Freya with equivalent English translations. She had begun to learn Arabic in 1926 from an old monk at San Remo and continued her lessons in London at the School of Oriental and African Studies the following year. Immediately afterwards she visited the Lebanon and spent the cold winter months studying at Brumana, in the hills above Beirut.

She had by now reached the full bloom of womanhood, had experienced the complex emotions of love, and had borne the pain of bereavement. She had nursed the sick and dying and, for two years after the Armistice, had helped her mother to run the silk-factory. This latter task could have been undertaken only with mixed feelings; the former she had found uplifting and enriching. Little more than a girl when she entered the Italian military hospital, Freya emerged from the war a grown woman, with definite, carefully evaluated opinions on subjects such as freedom, strife, love and death, politics and divinity. While remaining outwardly conventional, Freya Stark had developed intellectually as a radical, determined individualist. Moreover, she was charming and made friends easily. The combination was a potent one.

Cautioned, possibly even deterred by her parents' separation and by Vera's unhappy marriage, she remained single. She felt, as yet, probably unaware of the conflict marriage could create between domestic responsibilities and the desire for travel; nevertheless, she remembered the hurt of a broken engagement and had not met anyone who, in her eyes, could match the endearing qualities she had found in W. P. Ker.

After her sojourn in Lebanon, followed by a spring-time expedition through the Jebel Druze, Freya arrived eventually in Baghdad in 1929, aged thirty-six, too late to meet Gertrude Bell, the doyenne of woman Arabists, who had died there three years previously. Freya had been ill for two years with a stomach ulcer and suffered from poor circulation, yet always appeared small plateful. As the travellers ate, the household – a mother and six children, one an infant – looked on in silence. Freya wrote in *The Valleys of the Assassins:*

> 'Who could withstand so heart-rending a spectacle? . . . I pretended to be satisfied half-way through the microscopic meal, and the four little boys lapped up what remained. As for the daughter, she had already learnt what is what in this world. She neither got nor expected a share.'

Besides pleasure, her journeys brought inward peace, the true source of which she revealed in her second volume of autobiography, *Beyond Euphrates* (1951): 'But never for a moment, if one desires this true contentment, can one think in terms of this life only: the proportion with eternity must be kept.' Often she lived alone, as in the mud-built houses of Shibam, hundreds of miles from the 'titanic barriers' of the ocean and from other Europeans: a lonely woman in the hinterland of Arabia, yet feeling such security in the night's silence that she would refuse the offer of a guard and leave the door of her room unlocked.

During those pre-war travels in Persia and South Arabia, Freya twice fell ill and almost died. In Persia, an impulsive decision to reject hospital treatment in the plains and instead, for better or worse, remain among the mountains, ostensibly saved her life. She had found courage and a will to survive in memories of her father, now in Canada, to whom she had always been close. 'I must not die before him, I thought again and again and again, hoping to spare him a useless grief. And when I reached Teheran I found a letter, telling me of his death during those hours when I lay ill in the hills.'

In Shibam, she was fed and nursed through the second major illness by an ugly Hadhramaut servant named Salim. Heedless of medicine and rest, her strength continued to ebb away. Her heart almost stopped beating; her pulse appeared to fail. And yet, she did not die. She took refuge in Virgil instead of her customary embroidery, prudently rationing his verses, knowing that in the wilderness a little must go a long way. The poems soothed her: '. . . lovely images of sleep, of the quiet night and the resting earth. And I found, too, something greatly inspiring in his disinterested, pagan fortitude of death.'

The coming of the Second World War postponed further private travels. Freya's communicative talent, and her intimate knowledge of the Middle East and its languages, were seized upon by the Ministry of Information. She assisted the spread of propaganda, yet disliked and mistrusted the term which, she had discovered, no longer implied the broadcasting of genuinely held beliefs, but instead cloaked 'two opposite ideas, the truth and the hiding of the truth'. This war, like the work it forced upon her, caused Freya to reconsider and re-evaluate her individual moral stance with regard to patriotism and liberty, and indeed the very necessity for conflict. Patriotism, in those uncertain days, a sentiment so universally clung to and upheld, could scarcely be questioned in public. To do so would have cast grave doubts upon the questioner's loyalty to country and cause. Yet, Freya considered patriotism and its dependence upon geographical frontiers an arbitrary emotion, just as the years of travel had reinforced her belief in the similarities, rather than the differences, between peoples. Language, which she had found liable either to open or close the door on different races, more than anything, she concluded, 'circumscribes our freedom'.

Liberty had flowered among the nomad tribes as a tangible phenomenon, rather than a mere, theoretical concept. Freya would find it again after the war among the mountain ranges and along the rivers of the Eastern Mediterranean. As to her personal commitment to war itself, she wrote many years afterward: 'Action and inaction are merely two facets of activity, and when in danger it is better to hold a sharp knife by the handle rather than so to blunt it that no one, friend or foe, can find it useful.'

In an effort to gain support for Britain against the Italian forces menacing the Yemen, Freya agreed to travel secretly through the region to San'a, showing a motley series of propaganda films, which included the British Fleet at Spithead, an air-display, a cavalry charge at Aldershot and glimpses of daily life in Edinburgh! That such an oddly eccentric programme succeeded was due more to Freya's persuasive commentaries than any intrinsic qualities of its own. In carrying it out, Freya had been aware of the certain risk of reprisal by the Italian government and feared for her mother's safety at Asolo. Inevitably, Flora was arrested and imprisoned, but, due to the intervention of friends and considering her age and ill-health, she was spared a Fascist concentration camp and instead managed to reach the United States, where she died in 1942.

At the end of the war, Freya worked for several months in India as a personal assistant to the vicereine, Lady Wavell, after which she returned to Asolo. Two years later, she married Stewart Perowne, whom she had known in Aden and Baghdad. Her decision finally to marry was impulsive, the consequences unhappy for them both. After living together for six months in the Caribbean, where her husband had been posted by the Foreign Office, and later in Benghazi, the couple separated and Freya set up house once

more in Asolo.

She was by now well into her fifties, extremely active, at the summit of her artistic and intellectual powers. Wave upon wave of travels followed in Greece and Turkey. Freya journeyed along the Libyan coast and explored the deserts of Tunisia, in addition to visiting Sicily, Cyprus, Malta, Crete, Syria, Persia, Afghanistan, India, East Africa and China. She rode a pony in the footsteps of her antique hero, Alexander the Great, journeys described in *Alexander's Path* (1958); and from Lake Van negotiated the remote Hakkiari Mountains of Eastern Turkey, documenting her travels in a beautiful work of little more than a hundred pages entitled *Riding to the Tigris* (1959). Few of these post-war expeditions attained the prestige of her early travels in Persia and the Hadhramaut, however, and earlier volumes, *The Southern Gates of Arabia* (1936), *Seen in the Hadhramaut* (1938) and *A Winter in Arabia* (1940), represented a chapter of experience which would remain for ever closed, areas of the Arab world which Freya would not re-enter. These later writings, nevertheless, consolidated her literary reputation, and the income which they provided paid for the journeys themselves.

Freya still upheld her maxim of writing in order to travel, but not in order to live. This economic theory failed occasionally in practice, but generally helped to maintain the distinction between her worlds. Her writing would prove itself to be an artistic rather than a financial success; yet, given a bare minimum of the latter, she felt satisfaction in the former achievement. Today, aged eighty-nine, although she admits only with modest reluctance that her work has been decreed among the finest of its kind, she is frankly confident of her literary judgement.

Her success as a writer and traveller has won her many academic distinctions and honours: a D.Litt. from the University of Durham and an LL.D. from the University of Glasgow. In 1953 she was made a C.B.E.; in 1972 a D.B.E. and a Freeman of the City of Los Angeles. In 1949, she became a Sister of the Order of St John of Jerusalem. Dame Freya has been for many years one of a handful of Honorary Women Members of the Alpine Club, a privilege which delights her almost as much as the awards she received for early journeys in Luristan and the Hadhramaut: the Back Grant in 1933, the

Founder's Medal in 1942, both from the Royal Geographical Society; in 1951 the Percy Sykes Memorial Medal from the Royal Central Asian Society. In 1934 and 1956, she was presented with the Royal Asiatic Society's Triennial Burton Medal and the Mungo Park Medal from the Royal Scottish Geographical Society.

In 1970, Freya made the first of three mounted treks into the Himalayan foothills, which she approached through Western Nepal. In the winter of 1980, she travelled there by a different route, riding a sturdy, dark-brown Tibetan pony named Rati Gori, or 'Red Bells'. In February 1981, Red Bells again safely carried her up to the Tibetan border on an expedition filmed for television by the director Colin Luke, who also filmed Freya's nostalgic journey by raft down the Syrian Euphrates in 1977. She has felt no desire to write about these journeys, having abandoned literary work for the time being. An Afghanistan travelogue, *The Minaret of Djam*, and a further collection of essays, *A Peak in Darien*, were published in 1970 and 1976, respectively, in addition to eight volumes of her collected *Letters* between 1974 and 1982.

While she continues to travel and enjoys the prospect of a forthcoming adventure as much as ever, Freya is also content to live alone at Asolo, reading and re-reading in strict chronological sequence works which record the history of mankind from Sumerian times, through the Egyptian dynasties, the Greek and Roman Empires, to the Dark Ages, the Crusades and beyond. She has become less gregarious, although she is by no means unsociable. She exhilarates in serious conversation, but finds gossip on the whole stale and boring. More and more, her talk leans towards reflective and philosophical subjects, which is quite natural: nevertheless, contemplation has in no sense become a substitute for action in her life. As always, the two go together; only in recent years have their emphases begun to change.

Freya possesses great reserves of wisdom, humour and vitality. She is hospitable and welcoming. She still works hard, corresponding with friends and preparing for press the final volumes of her *Letters*. These Freya regards unpretentiously as a valuable insight into the social history of the past half-century. However, she makes it quite clear that they were never written with any thought of publication, many having been scribbled as she sat beside a ditch while her servants set up camp or cooked the evening meal. The impression given to modern readers of a deliberately polished form is, she maintains, due largely to the different, nowadays less exacting, use of language. Although Freya has been criticised for her 'purple passages' — and cheerfullly acknowledges their existence here and there in her work — she has invariably taken great

trouble to find words which express her meaning accurately. Acquaintances who have travelled with her and read descriptions of landscape which she jotted down in her notebook, perched on a rock or reclining in the shade of a tree, affirm that these have differed hardly at all from the published version. Her conversation, too, for all its bubbling spontanaeity, is habitually precise, the words carefully chosen, full of colour and lively atmosphere. The love of words is in her bones, as much as a deep respect for literature infuses her whole being. For this reason alone, it may be as a great writer who travelled in the East, rather than as a traveller who also wrote brilliantly on Eastern subjects, that Freya Stark will be best remembered.

The photographs which follow represent the third alternative means by which Freya has recorded her life and journeys. They provide a personal view, no less vivid than her books and letters, of countries and peoples, their costumes, architecture and archaeology. Freya's main artistic outlet has been words, yet her innate sense of form, structure and composition in space is revealed in the finest of many thousands of photographs taken with the rare miniature 35mm Leica camera, which she has used since 1933.

Photography occupied usually about a quarter of the entire time given to one of her expeditions. In the desert, she would rise an hour or two before dawn to develop films in her tent, while the air was still cool. Almost all her photographs she took herself; occasionally, however, she would carefully pre-set the Leica, then instruct a servant how to release the shutter, in order that she, too, might be included in the picture. A successful example of this method shows Freya, dressed in a straight skirt, carrying a handbag, marching through a rocky defile towards Petra where, she recalls gleefully, upon arrival she spent the night in a tomb! However, such photographs are exceptional and the entire collection of more than six thousand mounted prints, and perhaps five times as many negatives, contains few of the photographer herself.

Many of Freya's most successful, candid portraits were taken out-of-doors in the streets or in bazaars. Very often she would discover an interesting archway or perhaps a carved or painted door which she considered would frame a subject perfectly. She would then select the most favourable time of day, focus her camera on the chosen background and quite simply wait for a suitable subject to appear. Because she did not give the impression of aiming the camera directly *at* someone, but appeared instead to be photographing part of a building, she generally managed to obtain natural, unselfconscious results.

Among the most interesting photographs,

from an ethnographical point of view, are Freya's studies of women and girls. A number of these, taken in the *harim* before the last war, show the women unveiled, something no man could have achieved. Photographs of this kind, their artistic quality apart, have made a definite contribution to our knowledge of desert Arab life, and are historically valuable in consequence.

War, redevelopment, disruption of traditional ways of life in Arabia and elsewhere have swept away many fine, old buildings and drastically changed the character of towns and villages such as Kuwait and Abu Dhabi. Freya knew Kuwait over forty years ago when, in her own words, 'it was a dream of a little desert Arab town with sandy streets'. Expansion and reconstruction, financed by massive post-war oil revenues, have gradually eroded the desert heritage, replacing much that was representative, colourful and distinctive with a quasi-Western domestic and industrial environment, often characterless and incongruous. No matter how carefully Western planners might proceed, the damage caused by such historical and cultural dislocation cannot be satisfactorily repaired. Freya's photographs are therefore an important record of the traditional Arab world, much of which is now gone for ever.

Alexander Maitland

Asolo, February 1982

Lebanon, Palestine, Syria, Transjordan

'We came to a heavy studded door, on which he knocked: ten centuries dropped from me by magic: I should not have been at all surprised to see the Caliph and his two companions on the other side! The door was opened from the inside, and there was a great vaulted hall, lighted from a window in the roof, and with a cistern of flowing water in the centre. There were alcoves with carpets on a raised platform round three sides, and various men lying about on them with their heads wrapped in turbans and nothing much except their big bath wraps on. I did feel I was not in at all a suitable place! They gathered round me in an instant. Then I heard the door clank to behind me with a horrid sound as if a chain were dropped.'—Letters from Syria.

1 *Lebanon: Theatre at the ancient Phoenician coastal city of Byblos, 1958.*

2 *Lebanon: Ruined Corinthian capitals and fragment of a frieze, 1961.*

3 *Lebanon: Portico of the theatre, Baalbek, 1959.*

4 *Lebanon: Rooftop view over Tripoli, 1959.*

5 *Syria: Leading the pack-mules down a rocky hillside, 1939.*

6 *Syria: Jebel Druze, an elderly Druze of Lejja, 1928. Early in the 11th century, the Druzes ceased to be a religious sect, and the name afterwards signified a race or clan.*

7 *Syria: Camels carrying an enclosed woman's* howdah *on the road to Damascus, 1928. This shows how women of the* harim *were transported in privacy from place to place.*

8 *Syria: Damascus, the forecourt of the Great Mosque of the Omeyyades, 1928.*

9 *Palestine: Jerusalem, view across fields of olives to the Mosque of Omar, 1933.*

10 *Palestine: Jerusalem, the Jaffa gate, beside which, according to legend, lie the graves of the two brothers who built the city walls, 1933.*

10 *Palestine: Jerusalem, the Jaffa gate, beside which, according to legend, lie the graves of the two brothers who built the city walls, 1933.*

11 *Palestine: Jerusalem, a cobbled street, 1933.*

12 *Palestine: Banias, source of the River Jordan, 1931.*

13 *Palestine: Near Nazareth, a harvest scene with oxen, 1929.*

14 *Transjordan: Petra, the 'rose-red city', the remains of el Kazneh, called 'Pharaoh's Treasury' by the Bedouin who once believed that its stone urn contained gold, 1933.*

15 *Transjordan: Petra, entrance to the narrow chasm one-and-a-quarter miles long, known as el Siq, 1929.*

16 *Transjordan: Petra, el Siq, 1933.*

17 *Syria: Villes Mortes, near Dar Quita, 1956. Friends of the guides hold out bunches of spring flowers.*

18 *Syria: Villes Mortes, between Dar Quita and Babiska, showing continuous frieze detail at windows, 1956.*

19 *Syria: Villes Mortes, between Dar Quita and Babiska, detail of doorway, 1956.*

20 *Syria: Villes Mortes, the ruined 6th-century basilica of Qalb Lozé, 1956.*

21 *Syria: Villes Mortes, Qalb Lozé, the chevet, 1956.*

22 *Syria: Villes Mortes, 4th-century church and dovecote at Ruwaiha in the Jebel Barisha, North Syria, one of the oldest of these ruins, 1954.*

23 *Syria: Villes Mortes, 5th-century basilica, showing the arch construction, Ruwaiha, 1954.*

24 *Syria: Villes Mortes, the nave of a ruined 4th-century church, Ruwaiha, 1954.*

25 *Syria: The Crusader Castle of Sahyoun, west of Latakia, 1937.*

26 *Syria: The Castle of Sahyoun, the moat, 1939.*

27 *Syria: Qadmus, 1939.*

28 *Syria: Dana in the Jebel Riha, a house occupied by Dame Freya, 1956.*

29 *(Overleaf) Syria: Krak des Chevaliers, the most complete example of the Crusader Castles, near Homs, 1939. The name derives from* Hisn el-Akrad, *'Castle of the Kurds'; Akrad became Krat, afterwards Krak.*

30 *Syria: Krak des Chevaliers, view from the battlements at the first upper level, 1939.*

31 *Syria: Sheizar, a picturesque 12th-century Arab fortress, 1939.*

32 *Syria: Resafa, a biblical town in the Syrian desert south of the Euphrates, 1941.*

33 *Syria: Ramleh, the so-called 'Tower of the 40 martyrs', 1943. Actually it is the minaret of a 14th-century mosque built by Suleiman the Magnificent, which was turned by the Crusaders into a Christian Church.*

34 *Syria: Kal'a, Aleppo, 1954.*

35 *Syria: Alleiga Nosairi, 1939.*

36 *Syria: Baghuta, women and children, 1956.*

37 *Syria: Alleiga Nosairi, woman making butter, 1939.*

38 *Syria: El Bara, 1954.*

39 *Syria: Burj Duahakkan, one of Dame Freya's guides, 1956.*

40 *Syria: 'Shakespeare's fool', 1939. This man used to follow the caravan about and laughed at everything he saw.*

41 *Syria: Children near the ruins of Qalb Lozé, Villes Mortes, 1956.*

42 *Syria: Jezirá, cutting corn on the banks of the Euphrates, 1939.*

43 *Syria: Hama, a young acolyte with flowers, 1939.*

44 *Syria: Beggar and bystanders in the bazaar at Aleppo, 1939.*

45 *Syria: Interior of a tent in the Syrian desert, bedouin drinking coffee, 1937.*

46 *(Overleaf) Syria: South of the Euphrates, near Sirrin, bedouin crouched over a desert meal, 1939.*

47 *Syria: Latakia, 1939.*

48 *Syria: Euphrates ferry, 1939. Dame Freya spent three weeks in 1977 sailing down the Syrian Euphrates on a similar raft; the 1977 raft had a small reed shelter added.*

Iraq, Kuwait

'I was indeed surrounded by great kindness, and was very happy in my doll's house in the slum. A feeling of friendliness pervaded the whole street. It made a delightful contrast with the Baghdad newspapers, whose articles were chiefly anti-British at that time. We did not bother about nationalisms, and as for religions, I found every sect very pleasant if the other sect were not standing by. And people were extraordinarily kind. A very few days after my arrival, the blacksmith sent a message to say that he would try to work his fire only when I was out, as the fumes came curling up into my room. I used to leave my latchkey, which it was impossible to carry in anything except a small portmanteau, with the greengrocer. This horrified Marie, but pleased the Moslems—he being a Shi'a—though it was not so great a sign of confidence as I imagined, since I discovered later that all latchkeys in the neighbourhood opened anybody's front door indiscriminately, and I could always borrow a neighbour's if Marie happened to have carried mine off. Everyone was amused at my surprise over this arrangement. "You cannot expect every door to have a different sort of key?" they said.'—Baghdad Sketches.

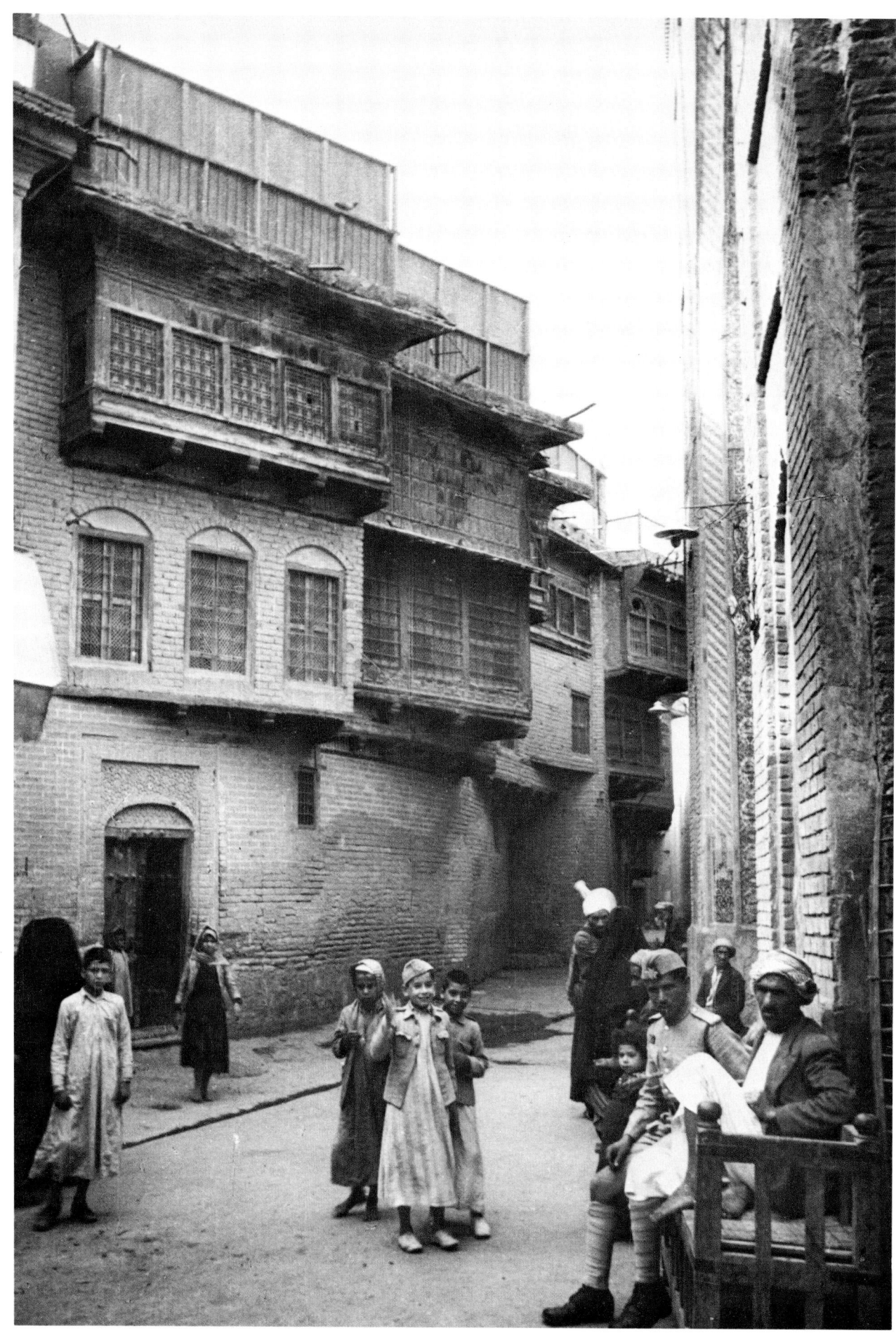

49 *Street in Kadhiman, a small town north of Baghdad on the west shore of the Tigris, 1941.*

50 *The desert west of Baghdad, 1957.*

51 *Baghdad, weavers, 1941.*

52 *Baghdad, interior of the suq, 1957.*

53 *Baghdad, a potter displays his wares, 1937.*

54 *The arch of Ctesiphon, near Baghdad, on the banks of the Tigris, 1957.*

55 *The arch of Ctesiphon, 1941. The entire façade was still standing as late as 1909.*

56 *Kerbala, the shrine, 1957.*

57 *A Rebaba player, 1957. The instrument had been made from half a paraffin-tin and a single horse hair.*

58 *The gardens of Kerbala, 1932.*

59 *A group of Kurdish tribesmen in a Baghdad street, 1932.*

60 *Threshing in Kurdistan, 1954.*

61 *A view of Akra, Kurdistan, 1954.*

62 *Hatra, slave-guard, 1942.*

63 *Anei'zah bedouin, holding a locally made rifle, 1954.*

64 *Street-scene in Nejf, 1937.*

65 *Ukhaidr, portrait of a slave-guard, 1957.*

66 *Marsh Arabs, or Madan, transporting cut reeds for buffalo-fodder, 1943. The Marshes of Iraq cover six thousand square miles and the Madan live in traditional reed-houses, built on tiny islands of floating vegetation.*

67 *Marsh Arab at a Euphrates ferry, 1943.*

68 *Marsh Arab mudhif, or guest tent, 1943.*

69 *One of the Muntafiq, Marsh Arab, 1937.*

70 *Yezidi feast, bringing the black bull to sacrifice, Shik Adi, 1957.*

71 *A Yezidi, 1957. The Yezidis are 'Devil-worshippers', who reverence the sun, fire, trees and fountains, make animal sacrifices and bury their dead facing the North Star.*

72 *Kuwait, shopping street, 1937.*

73 *Kuwait, bedouin harim, 1932.*

74 *Kuwait, fisherman, 1937.*

75 *Kuwait, slave-trader and* hadji, *1937.*

76 *A Shammar bedouin, 1941.*

Persia

'The valley was now full of loveliness. A last faint sense of daylight lingered in its lower reaches, beyond the village houses whose flat roofs, interspersed with trees, climb one above the other up the slope. Behind the great mountain at our back the moon was rising, not visible yet, but flooding the sky with gentle waves of light ever increasing, far, far above our heads. Here was more than beauty. We were remote, as in a place closed by high barriers from the world. No map had yet printed its name for the eyes of strangers. A sense of quiet life, unchanging, centuries old and forgotten, held our pilgrim souls in its peace.'—Valleys of the Assassins.

77 *The Parthian gate, Takht-i-Suleiman (the 'Throne of Solomon'), 1960.*

78 *Nishapur, patterns of sunlight and shadow in the gardens by Omar's tomb, 1969.*

79 *(Overleaf) Persepolis, 1960, 'the ancient Achaemenid Capital' described in 1628 by Sir Thomas Herbert as 'the only brave Antique-Monument (not in Persia alone) but through all the Orient'.*

80 *Persepolis gate, detail, 1959.*

81 *Persepolis gate, Xerxes' palace, detail of the Parthian tribute, 1959.*

82 *Mosque entrance doorway at Qum, detail, 1931.*

83 *Dezful, craftsman sewing water-skins, 1959. Two completed, decorated skins have been filled with water to prove his workmanship. Dezful signifies 'The Bridge Fort'.*

84 *(Overleaf) Isfahan, one of the ancient fairytale cities of Persia, covering twenty square miles in a mixture of splendour and decay, 1943.*

85 *Isfahan, showing its 'paved causeways', trees and a pool beside the Madraseh Mosque, 1943.*

86 *Shiraz, letter-writer with customers, 1969. Illiteracy has shown a tendency to rise, as the population of Eastern countries expands. Here the traditional occupation continues amidst Western symbols of materialism such as motor-cars and bicyles.*

87 *Kashgai women and children with their animals, near Persepolis, 1969.*

88 *Dilfard, nomad tents, 1959.*

89 *Dame Freya's muleteer and tethered pack-mule at a roadside* chaikhane, *or teahouse, 1931. The Persian word for tea,* chai, *occurs also in Swahili, as a result of the centuries old coastal trade with East Africa.*

90 Chaikhane, *interior, 1930*.

91 *Gazir Khan, 1930.*

92 *Traditional covered cart, pulled by four horses, 1931. The photographer has seen as many as six horses used.*

93 *Luristan, 1931. A Lur shepherd driving his flock. In 1933, Dame Freya received the Royal Geographical Society's Back Grant for her travels in this region.*

94 *A beggar, 1931.*

95 *Collectors of ransom at the Nihavend Pass into Khaveh, 1931.*

96 *Kurdish horseman from Urmiah, 1960. Note the foal standing behind him.*

97 *Women of Kalar Dasht, 1931.*

98 *Kharg island, Imamzade on site of fire-temple, 1959.*

99 *Kazvin, 1930.*

100 *Ice-storing houses near Yezd, 1943.*

101 *Village houses near Pasargade, 1959.*

102 *Pasargade, the tomb of Cyrus, 1959.*

South Arabia

'Zarathustra perhaps found in his words the secret of the wilderness. For it allows us to look for a while on our universe from a detatchment of loneliness; to weigh our values at leisure; to judge them anew in the presence of things almost eternal. Some we reject, and some we make our own: whatever the result of our weighing, ignoble it cannot be, thus born under the majestic visible eye of Time; we come back with a firmer step into the general world of men.'—Southern Gates of Arabia.

103 *The Red Sea, a small sailing vessel photographed from the deck of a steamer, 1940.*

104 *Aden, coastline pictured from fully rigged dhow, 1934.*

105 *Aden, dhows anchored in the harbour, 1940.*

106 *Aden, Somali woman carrying a water-jar, 1940.*

107 *Aden, sentry armed with a dagger and Lee-Enfield carbine, 1930.*

108 *Mukalla, the harbour, 1935.*

109 *(Overleaf) Wadi Hadhramaut, 1935.*

110 *Wadi Du'an, 1938.*

111 *Wadi Du'an, another view, 1935.*

112 *(Overleaf) Wadi Du'an, 1935. This photograph appears in* The Southern Gates of Arabia, *1936.*

113 *Masna'a in Du'an, 1935.*

114 *Hajarein in Du'an, 1935.*

115 *(Overleaf) The Sultan's palace, Seiun, 1935.*

116 *Pool in Sayyid Abu Bekr's garden at Seiun, 1936.*

117 *Seiun, detail of an arched doorway, 1938.*

118 *Shibam, on the southern fringes of the Empty Quarter, 1938. Bedouin drawing water from a well outside the town. Dame Freya suffered here from a near-fatal illness but was nursed back to health by a faithful servant.*

119 *Shibam, 1938, bedouin at a well.*

120 *Veiled ladies of the* harim, *Shibam, 1938. This photograph was used as a frontispiece in* A Winter in Arabia *(1940).*

121 *House-interior, Tarim, 1935.*

122 *Tarim, street-scene, 1935.*

123 *Tarim, market, a weaver selling decorated baskets, 1935.*

124 *(Overleaf) Huraidha, 1938.*

125 *The walls of Huraidha, 1938.*

126 *House-interior, Huraidha, 1938.*

127 *Huraidha, Mansab and his brother, friends of Dame Freya, 1938.*

128 *Huraidha, house-builder at work, 1938.*

129 *Shepherdesses, Huraidha, 1938. The wide-brimmed, conical hats are made of woven straw.*

130 *Huraidha, shepherdesses winnowing grain, 1938.*

131 *Huraidha, Mansabs of Meshed's tombs, 1935.*

132 *Huraidha, portrait of a litle girl wearing traditional head-dress and jewellery, 1938.*

133 *Huraidha, girl in traditional costume, 1938.*

134 *Camels and a guide on scree, near Huraidha, 1938.*

135 *Desert portrait taken on the way from Yeb'ett to Azzan, 1938.*

136 *Another portrait from the same area, 1938.*

137 *Yeb'ett Jol, road into the Hadhramaut, 1938.*

138 *Beiluim Rafiq, Wadi Hadhramaut, 1935. Note the shape and decoration of the locally manufactured rifle.*

139 *A multi-storey dwelling at Azzan, decorated with ibex-horns attached to brackets or set into the walls, 1938.*

140 *Lijlij, resting camels, 1938.*

141 *Bedouin loading a camel, 1938.*

142 *Camel-men of the Jol, 'Amd, 1939.*

143 *The caravan ready for departure, Wadi Meife'q, 1938.*

144 *Camels feeding during a desert halt on the way from Jol to Yeb'ett, 1938.*

145 *A riding-camel, showing the saddle and harness, 1938. Nowadays it would be almost impossible to find a riding-saddle in use anywhere in Arabia, so swiftly has this traditional means of transport declined.*

146 *Dhala, Jews, 1939.*

Turkey

'I never lay down to rest without a thought of gratitude and wonder for the goodness of the Turkish peasants as I found them. The Arabs and Greeks have more aristocratic virtues that lead to enterprise and hatreds and adventures based on exclusion. Goodness, since it is based on sharing, can never be aristocratic, and the Turkish villagers in their poverty are ready to share with all. The simplicity of their goodness is touching—its anxiety to help, its honourableness and active kindness, its love for children and flowers. Unlike most of the world, they do not undervalue their own—but show ready pleasure if any poor possession, air, view, or water, or any attractiveness in the hard and simple life is praised. They turn willingly from all their own distresses, delighted with whatever the humble excellence may be. Nor can I remember, during all my three visits to Turkey, to have been offended by a discourteous word.'—Alexander's Path.

147 *Istanbul, minarets at the Galata Bridge, 1963. The Galata Tower overlooks the Golden Horn; Galata is a suburb of Istanbul.*

148 *Istanbul, the walls of Theodosius, 1963. These walls commemorate the dynasty founded when Gratian invested Theodosius with the Imperial Purple.*

149 *Istanbul, half-ruined wooden houses built inside the West Wall, 1963.*

150 *Istanbul, the 'Sublime Porte', 1958.*

151 *View through the valley leading to Gümüs Han, 1958.*

152 *Sea of Marmara, 1960. On the undulating hills, new trees have been planted.*

153 *(Overleaf) The Castle of Hoshab, 1954; literally 'The Good Water', it overlooks the southern road running through the Zab Valley, to the east of Lake Van.*

154 *The Castle of Anamur, called Staméné by the Crusaders, on the southernmost cape of Turkey, facing Cyprus.*

155 *Anamur, a view from the battlements, out to sea.*

156 *Tombs of Demre, 1956.*

157 *Ürgüb, so-called 'fairy chimneys' in the Göreme valley, Cappadocia, 1962.*

158 *(Overleaf) Ürgüb, 1962.*

159 *The Church of St Sophia, Trebizond, 1958. Now a museum like St Sophia in Istanbul, it is one of the rare examples of Christian architecture remaining outside the capital.*

160 *A reed-thatched house in Caria, 1957.*

161 *Wooden house built on the edge of woodland near Ören, 1957.*

162 *Traditional wooden house, Istanbul, 1962. Examples of this type of building are becoming fewer.*

163 *A plateau cart with solid wheels, from the Elmali plateau of Lycia, south-west Turkey, 1952.*

164 *Pause at a Harput inn, 1954.*

165 *Gypsy playing a reeded pipe on the roadside leading to Maraş, 1954. The name 'Maraş' is of Hittite origin.*

166 *A shepherdess at Sagalassus (now known as Ağlason), 1954.*

167 *A peasant playing his lute outside his cottage in the Xanthos Highlands, 1954.*

168 *Woman drawing water from a well near Dara, 1954.*

169 *Water-seller, Maradan, 1954.*

170 *Letter-writer with a client, Bursa, 1957. It is interesting to note that this man has updated his calling by abandoning the pen for a typewriter.*

171 *Vanishing modes of transport, Bursa, 1957.*

172 *Vanishing modes of transport, Büjük Ada, Istanbul, 1963.*

173 *Vanishing modes of transport, Finike, 1952.*

174 *Little boys near Ankara, 1954.*

175 *A family group at Halfete, on the Euphrates, 1961. The hard life of these poor people shows in their faces and the woman looks much older than her years.*

176 *The photographer's shadow near a group in the market place at Balik-i-Shihu, 1962.*

177 *(Overleaf) The Hakkiari mountains, tents of Soma, 1958. This photograph appears in* Riding to the Tigris *(1959.)*

178 *Hakkiari, 1958. These women weavers are seated on the ground with their looms stretched over a shallow depression which allows freedom of movement; in fact, the exact reverse of a table.*

179 *Weavers working in the shade, Soli, 1954.*

180 *Amasya, wooden bridge on Roman piers, 1962. On the hill are Pontic tombs and the ruins of the Citadel.*

181 *Massive piers of a bridge at Bursa, 1957.*

182 *A graceful arch spans the river at Batman Su, 1954.*

183 *Sinop, 1958.*

184 *Istanbul, Anatoli Hissar (The Castle of Asia), 1966.*

185 *Old, decorated craft on the shores of the Bosphorus, 1956.*

186 *Giresun, a cargo of sheep and water-jars at the harbour, 1958.*

187 *Cotton-gatherers in peaceful surroundings at evening, 1952.*

Egypt

'Very few tourists have any idea how agreeable the Egyptian country is; neither have the Egyptians, at any rate in the north, and you would think them unaware of anything between Cairo in winter and Alexandria in summer. It would perhaps be a blessing for the landlords themselves if their incomes were so reduced as to make it advisable for them to live in some garden beside their own brown villages, where the water buffaloes come slowly home along the tow path by canals in the sunset light, and the date harvest ripens in brazen clusters, avenues of Byzantine carved capitals close to the columns of their trees, whose serrated spiked fronds above are motionless and sharp against the sky.'—East is West.

188 *Tel el Kebir, 1941. A falconer offers food to one of his charges.*

189 *Tel el Kebir, 1941. A mounted falconer carries a hooded falcon on his wrist.*

190 *Tel el Kebir, 1941. Another portrait of the same man, showing the falcon and the horse's decorated bridle in greater detail.*

191 *Pool at Mohammed Ali's palace, Shubra, 1941.*

192 *Cairo, Bab al Nasir, 1956.*

193 *A street in Maristan, Cairo, 1940.*

194 *Maristan, street-scene, 1956.*

195 *Cairo, craftsmen engraving brass trays, 1961.*

196 *Muski, Cairo, street-scene, 1961. The Muski quarter, formerly known as the Frank, then the Rosetti, quarter, was named after Iz ed Din Musk, a relation of Saladin, who built the Muski Bridge over the canal.*

197 *Qarafa, the City of the Dead, the cemetery on the south side of Cairo, near the Citadel, 1961.*

198 *The Nile at Cairo, 1940.*

199 *A sphinx at the ruins of Memphis, a few miles south of Cairo, 1940.*

200 *El Karnak, 1941.*

201 *Edfu, panel, 1941. Miracle plays known as 'The Mysteries of Isis', dealing with subjects such as life, death and mummification, in mimicry, were performed at certain temples, including Edfu.*

202 *(Overleaf) The Nile at Luxor, 1941.*